Newcas
FRAME *by* FRAM

C000071432

A sophisticated shopping centre, an atmospheric party city and a hotbed of football mania – that's Newcastle today.

But for a couple of thousand years it was a wild frontier town, so bad in Roman times they had to build a massive wall to keep out the constant raiders from up North.

Underneath a railway bridge close to the dramatic Castle Keep, modern paving stones mark the outline of a number of small rooms of what was once a Roman garrison building. One of these rooms was the office of the garrison commander of the depot, Pons Aelius, serving the building of the Roman Wall.

It is believed that, around 120 AD, the Emperor Hadrian actually visited that room when he arrived on the banks of the Tyne to survey the progress of his great venture. Aelius was the Hadrian family name.

Just a matter of yards away, on the site of what is now the ingenious Swing Bridge, there would have stood a substantial Roman Bridge. The Swing Bridge, designed by Lord Armstrong, was opened in 1876 and was driven by hydraulic power.

Obviously, much has changed since those far-off days but now when you talk about Newcastle you are actually talking about Tyneside and the North East.

Foreigners, by that I mean non-Geordies, associate Newcastle with coal and shipbuilding but the pits were spread over a wide area of Durham and Northumberland and the shipyards straddled the River Tyne for mile after mile, after leaving the bounds of the city.

But the Toon, a city of bridges, markets and imposing streets and buildings, embodies the Geordie spirit and is regarded as the capital of the region.

Heritage Editor: Harri Aston
Written and compiled by: Ray Marshall
Designer: Ben Renshaw

Part of the Lost Britain **Collection**
© 2013 Trinity Mirror. All Rights Reserved

Managing Director: Ken Rogers
Senior Editor: Steve Hanrahan
Senior Art Editor: Rick Cooke
Editor: Paul Dove
Senior Marketing Executive: Claire Brown
Photosales: 0845 300 3021
Images: Mirrorpix, PA Photos
Printed by: William Gibbons

Chemical threat Newcastle Chronicle and Journal staff wearing gas masks as part of air raid precautions, pictured in about 1940

Fighting spirit that defied the Nazis

Newcastle and its people took a terrible toll in the Second World War. The home front was also the frontline and civilians had to shoulder the terrifying ordeal of air raids

Compared to other major cities, Nazi air raids on Newcastle and Tyneside during the Second World War could never be described as a blitz, which was surprising because the shipbuilding, armaments factories and heavy engineering associated with the area was well documented. But there were still a great number of tragedies that hit the area.

It is also strange to remember a tunnel, which was built in Victorian times and ran for two miles under the city of Newcastle, was one of Tyneside's main defences against German air raids during the Second World War.

The Victoria Tunnel was started in 1839 and engineered to carry coal from the outskirts of the city down to the riverside. The tunnel was sealed up in 1860 and has never been reopened, except as an air raid shelter during the war, when up to 9,000 people could shelter at any one time.

But Tyneside never escaped from its share of tragedies at the hands of the Luftwaffe. More than a hundred men, women and children were killed when a German raid struck Wilkinson's Lemonade factory in North Shields – whole families were wiped out on Saturday, May 3, 1941 as a direct hit sent the heavy machinery down into the basement which served as an air raid shelter. Although 195 people were taking shelter there that night, many had refused to use the factory because of safety concerns but those down in that basement would have felt safe and were said to be singing and in quite a jolly mood.

But out of tragedy came heroism and lucky escapes. Survivors remembered the shelter's ARP Warden, Ellen Lee. Suffering burns, she put herself in extreme danger in helping to rescue 32 people.

Mrs Lee's son, Albert, who was 17 at the time, later recalled: "That night I was in the shelter with my sister, Hilda. We were sitting on the bunks in Room No 1. The shelter had a lot of people in but it was fairly quiet, no music, just people chatting. When the bomb hit I heard a dull 'bonk' sound.

"Then everything went black and people started screaming. I shouted 'Don't strike a bloody match' – I was thinking there might have been a gas leak.

"And then my mother (Mrs Lee) told everyone to follow her torch light. The exit was blocked but she just shoulder-charged the wall until it gave way. She got over 30 people out. I was unharmed but my sister was in a bad way. She had a big wound in her side and a broken arm and leg. My father didn't even recognise her when he came to Kettlewell School where the injured were taken. The woman sitting opposite me . . . well, there wasn't much left of her."

Another report of that night said wardens running to the scene found a baby lying in the street. The baby had been blown out of the factory but miraculously lay there unharmed.

There was heavy loss of life in the Market Square at South Shields and places such as Matthew Bank and Gibson Street in Newcastle as the German raids struck home.

Tyneside was ablaze in 1942 when Manors Goods Yard suffered direct hits and fires, which lasted for days, lit up Tyneside at night and the smell of burning sugar pervaded the city.

But it wasn't all one-way traffic. In August 1941 the Germans did attempt a mass attack on the North East, with Tyneside thought to be their particular target. Unfortunately for them, many of the squadrons protecting London were sent to the North East for rest periods – imagine the surprise of the Luftwaffe pilots who had been told the area was only lightly defended, only to be confronted by frontline and battle-experienced pilots only too eager to exact revenge for earlier raids.

The Germans suffered such massive losses that they never again attempted a big daylight raid over the area.

Thousands of Tyneside children were evacuated to country villages where they could continue their school work unhampered. But separation from their families proved too much for many who were soon back home on Tyneside – they would rather brave the German raids than live apart from their families.

But of those who did not return there were differing stories. Some had the time of their lives and formed long-lasting friendships, while others felt they were just used as a way of getting cheap labour for the farms.

▲ **Fighting posties** *Post Office members of the Home Guard on Sunday morning parade at the Orchard Street sorting office in February 1941*

▶ **Mind your head** Storekeepers checking some of the 19,000 new-type steel helmets which arrived in Newcastle for distribution to street fire watchers on March 26, 1941

◀ **Dark days** The Lord Mayor of Newcastle (Councillor A D Russell) inspecting men of the Home Guard attached to an engineering establishment in the North East on August 13, 1940

▶ **Homes hit** Severely damaged houses in High Heaton, Newcastle, after a German air raid in September 1940

Horrific damage Pictured is the LNER Goods Station, New Bridge Street, the morning after an attack on September 2, 1941

▲ **Pre-war planning** Residents of Links Avenue, Monkseaton, who decided to construct their own communal air raid shelter. They are pictured here at work on the first trench on August 30, 1939

▲ **Getting ready** Work in progress on September 13, 1939, on one of the air raid shelters being constructed by Newcastle authorities for residents of Noble Street, 10 days after the start of the war. The shelter was constructed in the centre of the roadway and entrances were to be from the traffic islands

◀ **Well prepared** Work is pushed ahead on the group of ARP air raid shelters at the Vickers-Armstrong Scotswood works in Newcastle, months before the war had even started. This picture was taken on April 16, 1939

Hostilities end *Miss Eleanor Vallans, of Robs Haugh Farm near Ponteland, carves a Christmas turkey for five German POWs on December 12, 1946. Her brother, Charles is second from the right*

Fire worries *By 1941 many Newcastle firms, like this one on City Road, were adopting 24 hour fire-watching with use of roof spotters*

▶ **Public protection** *The picture shows the air raid shelter sign on Northumberland Street, December 14, 1939*

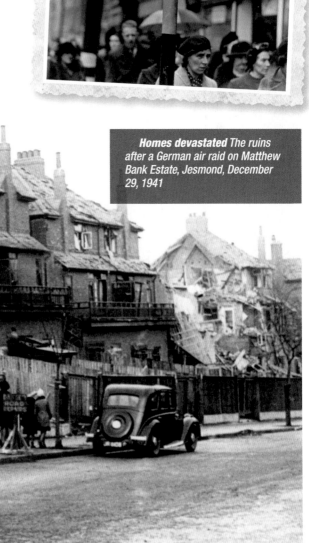

Homes devastated *The ruins after a German air raid on Matthew Bank Estate, Jesmond, December 29, 1941*

Vanquished enemy *A shot down German Messerschmitt Bf 109 fighter aircraft. It is seen here at Blyth's Market Place for the town's War Weapons Week on January 28, 1941*

▲ **Blooming marvellous**
The Best-Kept Gardens contest for the Condercum Estate, Newcastle, brought to light a new angle on gardening – how to make the ARP Anderson shelter a 'thing of beauty'. This picture in Westholme Gardens shows how it could be done. Pictured on August 11, 1939

▶ **Heart wrenching** *One of the children evacuated during the war*

Any old iron? *The children of Temple Green, Gateshead, were enthusiastic collectors of scrap metal for the salvage campaign during the Second World War. So successful were they that this wagon was sent to bring their collection to the campaign's headquarters on August 20, 1940*

▲ **Collective spirit** *Volunteer workers prepare a meal for families rendered homeless by an air raid on the North East on Thursday, October 2, 1941*

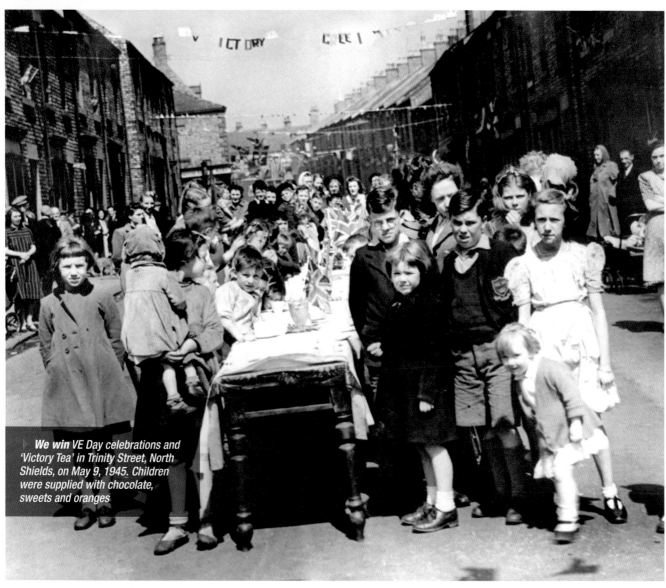

We win *VE Day celebrations and 'Victory Tea' in Trinity Street, North Shields, on May 9, 1945. Children were supplied with chocolate, sweets and oranges*

Birth of a ship The launch of the 115,000-ton tanker Nacella at Swan Hunter shipyard on March 28, 1968

Majestic wonders built on the Tyne

Some of the greatest names in British sea-faring history were constructed at the famous Tyneside yards, and they thrilled all who saw them

There she goes One of the greatest liners ever launched on the Tyne, Mauretania, enters the river at the Swan Hunter shipyard, Wallsend, on September 20, 1906.

FROM ocean-going liners to quarter-of-a-million-ton oil tankers, from famous battleships to the smallest yachts, we built them on the Tyne and they carried Geordie workmanship to the four corners of the Earth.

Ships had been launched on the River Tyne for centuries before the revolution of iron shipbuilding of the 19th century. John Coutts, who opened a yard at Low Walker, Newcastle, in 1840 was among the earliest pioneers in this field.

His ships included the Prince Albert, a paddle steamer, and the QED, an iron sailing collier which was equipped with an engine linked to a screw propeller. Another pioneer, Charles Mitchell, also began operating a yard at Low Walker in 1852.

His yard was to play a leading role in the development of oil tanker design. It launched the prototype of the modern ocean-going tanker, the Gluckhauf, in 1886. Other vessels produced in Mitchell's yard included Russian icebreakers, such as the Yermack and Angara, and train ferries.

In 1833, Mitchell's business merged with Lord Armstrong's giant armaments company at Elswick and the joint enterprise went from strength-to-strength. Soon, the new company of Armstrong Mitchell was building warships at Elswick while the Low Walker yard concentrated mainly on merchant vessels.

The Japanese Imperial Navy was among a host of customers to come to Elswick from abroad for cruisers and battleships. During the 1880s and 1890s the yard became renowned for its fast and well-produced cruisers. Many of the cruisers which fought for Japan in their crushing naval victory against Russia at the Battle of Tsushima in 1905 had been born at Elswick.

The world-renowned company of Swan Hunter began operations at the Wallsend shipyard under the title CS Swan and Co in 1874. Its most illustrious ship, the Cunard passenger liner Mauretania completed in 1907, held the Blue Riband for the fastest Atlantic crossing longer than any other ship and was recognised the finest example of the Tyne's shipbuilding skills. In 1903, Swan Hunter merged with the neighbouring firm of Wigham Richardson, which opened the Neptune Yard at Low Walker.

Warships, tankers, cargo carriers, ferries, passenger ships and cable-laying and repair ships were among the great variety of vessels launched. But shipbuilding was not confined to the north bank of the Tyne.

Firms on the southern shore included the Jarrow yard founded by Charles Palmer and his brother George in 1851. Their second ship, the John Bowes of 1852, was the Tyne's first successful iron-built steam collier. There followed many other orders for similar colliers. Palmer's yard also launched many merchant vessels and received orders for warships from the Royal Navy. Also on the south bank, the Redheads yard at South Shields made a major contribution to the world's trade by producing many tramp steamers, as well as numerous general cargo ships. Hawthorn Leslie's Hebburn Yard was also a south side outfit with a leading role.

In 1907, the production of vessels built by Swan Hunter and Wigham Richardson amounted to 15% of the world's total tonnage that year. It exceeded the total output of Holland, Spain and Japan. And these are the figures from just one of the Tyne's builders.

In 1913, the Armstrong industrial empire, by then known as Armstrong Whitworth, opened the Walker Naval Yard.

The Depression of the early 1930s witnessed the near collapse of the river's shipbuilding industry and mass unemployment. The closure of Palmers at Jarrow brought great economic suffering and shocked the nation. The Second World War revived the fortunes of the Tyne's shipyards. Its workforces were kept busy on new warships, repairs, refits and replacements for vessels sunk. The return of peace in 1945 again brought a host of orders but the boom was short-lived.

Today, shipbuilding has disappeared from the Tyne. Like the coal industry, it has been wiped off the map of the North East.

Famous ship The Mauretania, which would go on to hold the Blue Riband for the fastest crossing of the Atlantic by a passenger vessel, was built on the Tyne

▲ **New era** The supertanker Esso Hibernia being fitted out after its launch on the River Tyne at Swan Hunter on November 19, 1970. It was one of a series of supertankers whose massive size and design was a result of the Suez Crisis and the closing of the Suez Canal

▼ **Modern war machine** The aircraft carrier HMS Ark Royal under construction at Swan Hunter shipyard in Wallsend, May 18, 1981. It was launched a few weeks later on June 2, 1981

▲ **Time for trials** In this splendidly atmospheric photograph, the newly-completed Mauretania moves down the Tyne on the afternoon of October 22, 1907. It was escorted by tugs and on its way to Cunard in Liverpool as part of its official trials

▲ **Waving off**
A crowd of locals turned out to see off a supertanker on its maiden voyage. The small band of residents turned out, despite the wet and windy weather, to wave off the World Unicorn, Swan Hunter's 257,000-ton tanker. The tanker was heading out to take part in two weeks of trials in the North Sea

▲ **More than a ship** This 400ft floating dock, built by Swan Hunter and Wigham Richardson, left the Wallsend shipyard for Apapa. The 4,000-ton dock, for the Nigerian Port Authority, was completed in 1961

Crowd favourite Crowds gathered on the banks of the River Tyne to watch the Esso Northumbria sail down the river, heading for the North Sea to do its sea trials on February 9, 1970

◀ *Childhood memories* Two young fans greet Princess Anne with flags on her visit to Tyneside to launch the tanker World Unicorn

On its way The 400ft floating dock leaving for Nigeria in 1961

On their way in Their strike over, shipyard men return to work at Wallsend shipyard in 1957

Job well done Shipyard workers stream home in 1906 with the Mauretania on the Tyne behind them

On their way out Shipyard workers finished for the night after their shift in 1957

Industrial strife A mass meeting of Tyneside shipyard workers in protest at the Government's Industrial Relations Bill in January 1971

▲ *Long walk* Tyneside shipyard workers head home in the 1950s

▲ These girls were working in a Wallsend shipyard, believed to be around 1930. On the far right is Mary Anne McNeil (maiden name Kirsop). The women were sent in to clean the ships out after they were launched or re-fitted

War duties Women workers next to a camouflaged ship at the Palmers shipyard during the Second World War

Bright lights *It was nearing midnight and although thousands had gone home, many were still enjoying all the fun of the fair at the Hoppings in 1956 at the Town Moor*

Fun-filled days at the Hoppings fair

A mix of magic, danger and excitement attracted millions of people to Newcastle's Town Moor – no matter what the weather

Roll up . . . roll up . . . and enjoy all the fun of the fair. And that's what Geordies have been doing for well over a 100 years.

To them the Hoppings was a place of magic, danger, excitement – there was the waltzer, the dive bomber, the big wheel, the cyclone and the wall of death where motorcyclists took danger to the very edge and frequently ended up in hospital.

There were the dodgems, the ghost train, boxing booths and the dancing girls and not forgetting the freak shows, including the bearded woman and the goat with five legs, Frankenstein's Castle, Skyliners and the house of crazy mirrors.

They all – and more – came to Newcastle's Town Moor for a week every June, attracting millions of North East fun-seekers, rain or shine – more often rain than shine.

In its heyday you could ride the biggest and most dangerous rides in Europe, see the snake man, ride the spinning Octopus and even put on a pair of boxing gloves before doing battle in a boxing ring.

And, if you were lucky enough to survive all that, you might be heading home eating fish and chips and clutching a coconut in one hand, a teddy bear in another and desperately trying to hang on to a water-filled bag carrying a terrified-looking gold

fish. The Hoppings, billed as Europe's biggest travelling fair, originated in 1892 as a Temperance Festival, in a bid to beat the drunkenness on the streets of Tyneside, before becoming a full-blown travelling fair which attracted the biggest shows from around Britain and Europe.

The first attractions were mostly military displays (cavalrymen slicing lemons with swords with horses at the gallop) and kite flying. This seems to have got off to a flying start as crowds of up to 150,000 attended in a week – three times more than attended the previous biggest Temperance Festival, a mere 48,000 at Crystal Palace.

Eventually, the modern-day Town Moor Hoppings was said to be two miles long of shows with crowds four and five deep. Its greatest enemy was the weather and the rain in particular, although the crowds just put on their wellies and came all the same.

But sadly we may have seen the last of this great spectacle because of bickering between the Freemen of Newcastle, who are responsible for the Town Moor and the Showmen's Guild. Will our children and grandchildren not get the chance to enjoy the delights and excitement that we tasted that great week every June on the Town Moor?

▲ *Fair scene*
Visitors looking out for the attractions at the Hoppings in June 1960

▶ *In the picture*
Photographer Chris Steele-Perkins' exhibition, England, My England, in 1969

▲ **Full house** Just look at the concentration on the faces of these women playing bingo in 1957

◄ **In a spin** Having fun on the waltzer in 1971

▲ Massive attraction *Thousands of people are captured in this image of the fair taken in 1960*

◀ Mystery show *Crowds enjoy the entertainment on offer in 1960*

▲ **Hold tight** These two thrill-seekers have fun on a ride in 1971

▶ **Good catch**
Four youngster
display their prize
goldfish in 1975

What's going on? Curious crowds pass the sideshows at the Hoppings in 1965

Wild time The Wild West Show is about to get under way and the performers are trying to attract the customers inside in 1947

▲ **Tastes good** These two youngsters enjoy some candy floss in June 1971

◀ **Round and round** It's fast but it doesn't seem a bit frightening for these fair-goers in 1969

End of the night *The crowds at the Hoppings in 1971 are now thinning out as the evening starts drawing to a close*

▲ **Flying high** *Two girls enjoy flying through the air at the Hoppings in 1975*

Showtime *One of the sideshows at the Hoppings in 1957*

High note *Geordie supergroup Lindisfarne playing a Christmas concert at Newcastle City Hall on December 20, 1980*

The soundtrack to Tyneside's life

Geordies have enjoyed watching the greatest acts of the day in Newcastle, and local bands and artists have thrilled people throughout the world with their music

THEY have all played Tyneside, from the Beatles to the Stones, from David Bowie to Springsteen, even local superstars such as Sting and Neil Tenant of the Pet Shop Boys – but however mega these names are, it is Lindisfarne's Christmas shows which are local legend.

Lindisfarne evolved from school bands and intermixed through their early teens before the Seventies supergroup emerged. Their story actually began in the early Sixties. Drummer Ray Laidlaw helped form the Aristokrats with Si Cowe and they played regularly around Tynemouth. Ray Laidlaw moved on to The Druids, who quickly developed a good sound through regular local gigs.

There were many name and line-up changes until they came to Downtown Faction.

At that time, Downtown Faction were Rod Clements, Ray Laidlaw, Si Cowe, Jeff Sadler and Richard Squirrel and they were getting a sizeable reputation. By 1967 they were getting fees of £15 for playing the Lacarno Ballroom, in Sunderland, and they were also playing the Quay Club, in Newcastle, and the Cellar Club in South Shields.

Eventually, Richard Squirrel was replaced in the line-up by Ray Jackson.

"The first time I met Jacka," said Ray "was at art college in Chillingham Road. I was going out for my lunch one day and I heard this amazing harmonica playing coming from the other end of the corridor. There he was in the common room playing an amazing harmonica. He was in a band called the

Autumn States and, ultimately, we nicked him with an offer he couldn't refuse."

Downtown Faction changed their name to Brethren but still found the going hard.

A new force was emerging on Tyneside at the time – Alan Hull. Alan was also gaining a reputation nationally. Eventually, after a bit of wooing, Alan performed with the Brethren at the Lampglass in Ashington.

Ray said: "I can remember the first time we did Lady Eleanor together and when we finished the song, I just knew. I said, 'That's it - we've cracked it'."

Then the final piece of the jigsaw dropped into place while they were making the album, Nicely Out Of Tyne, when they decided to change their name to Lindisfarne.

At the end of a tour in 1970, Lindisfarne returned to Newcastle to perform a Christmas show at the City Hall. They didn't realise it but it was the start of a long tradition. At the end of 1973 the band split while Alan Hull and Ray Jackson recruited new members for Lindisfarne Mark II. In 1975 Alan and Ray decided to call it a day and the original members got together for a reunion Christmas show at the City Hall. The following year they got together again for a "one-off" Christmas concert.

This was repeated every year until 1978 when the band decided to reform. These Christmas concerts are now legendary on Tyneside and continued for many years.

▲ *Song on the Tyne* Sailing down the Tyne on a on March 4, 1979 are, from left, Lindisfarne members Ray Jackson, Rod Clements, Si Cowe, Ray Laidlaw and Alan Hull

▲ *Seventies superstars*
It's mayhem as the Bay City Rollers perform at Newcastle City Hall in May 1975. The Evening Chronicle compared it to scenes 10 years earlier when the Beatles and Stones were on Tyneside

◄ *Hero worship*
Hands stretch up from the audience as Bay City Rollers fans try to get near to their heroes

▶ **Festive tradition** Lindisfarne's Ray Jackson, Rod Clements, Alan Hull, Ray Laidlaw and Si Cowe performing at Newcastle City Hall on December 11, 1985

▲ **Christmas cracker** Lindisfarne perform their first Christmas show at Newcastle City Hall in 1976, at the start of a legendary series of gigs

▶ **New era** Mick Jones (guitar) and Paul Simonon (bass) of the legendary Clash at the Students' Union in Newcastle on May 20, 1977

◄ **Freak out**
Fans get into the spirit of the Rolling Stones concert at Newcastle City Hall in March 1971

▶ **Superstar show** Performing on stage are Bill Wyman and Mick Jagger in 1971

Rock legend Singer Bob Dylan in concert at St James' Park on July 5, 1984

Beatlemania *It's October 1963 and long lines of Beatles fans queue around the corner from Newcastle City Hall in the attempt to get tickets to see the band*

▲ **Hide your love away**
Beatles fans read about their heroes as they queue for tickets in 1963

▶ **Fab four** *Paul, John, George and Ringo in Newcastle on January 29, 1964*

The king of Queen Freddie Mercury, right, on stage with drummer Roger Taylor and guitarist Brian May at St James' Park

Going Gaga The fans enjoy the brilliance of Queen at St James' Park in 1986

Heart of glass Debbie Harry of Blondie performs in concert at Newcastle City Hall on January 4, 1980

Grim job *Injured miners from the Easington Colliery disaster are carried from the pit by rescuers in 1951*

Dangerous job for proud community

The pits may have closed but within living memory this region was defined by the coal mining industry that powered a nation

Although "Coals to Newcastle" is still a widely used saying, it's all change today as we have to import all our coal after the mass closure of all local coalfields.

Many of our once-thriving coal towns are now little more than ghost villages.

In their heyday, pits abounded all over Northumberland and Durham, employing thousands and supporting a host of industries and shops – but now that is all a distant memory.

Originally, coal was excavated from open sites right next to the River Tyne, making it easy to transport to Newcastle and, from there, to be shipped all over the country by sea – an important part of the industrial revolution.

Of course, it was the rich merchants, land owners and particularly the church which made vast profits from the coal trade, especially when the open sites next to the river were spent and deeper mines further into Northumberland and Durham became the focus. Villages and collieries sprung up and labour moved from the towns and farms for this well paid but dangerous new lifestyle.

New workers came to the North East coal fields from Scotland, Ireland and all parts of England in search of work.

But all too frequently there were tragedies and great loss of life, despite regular reforms, which seemed to favour the coal owners more than the miners themselves. Because of the constrained working conditions down pits, children were an important part of the workforce – something which eventually jerked the national conscience as many perished in the disasters.

In 1947 the mines were nationalised and brought under Government ownership, and the power of the mining industry passed from the coal barons into the hands of the workers and the trade unions.

Inflation and fuel crises in the 1970s brought political power and influence to the miners' unions, who were able to resist Government attempts to transform the industry. Conflict, through strikes and massive demonstrations, dominated the industry until the orchestrated campaign by the Thatcher Government to finally smash the power of the unions, ultimately leading to the disintegration of the entire industry.

As mines closed, pit villages suffered because of the loss of wages. Today there are no true working mines left in the North East and 'Coals to Newcastle', especially from Eastern Europe is now the order of the day.

▲ *The last shift*
Miners coming off the last ever shift at Vane Tempest Colliery, Seaham, County Durham, June 1993

Home front Miners' cottages at North Seaton Colliery, Ashington

THIS COLLIERY IS NOW MANAGED BY THE **NATIONAL COAL BOARD** ON BEHALF OF THE PEOPLE

◀ **For the people** Nationalisation of the coal mines was hugely popular after it was introduced by the Attlee Government

◀ **Learning the job** Miners at work in an outside "practice" pit, in October 1959

▶ **Tough lives** A group of miners at Chester Moor Colliery in 1901

▼ **Weekend work** Miners leave Ravensworth Colliery near Birtley after a Saturday morning shift in January 1951

Work entrance Miners are seen at the entrance to the drift before entering the Coalcleugh mine at Allendale, near Hexham, in May 1950

End of the line *A sad moment as miners for the last time hang up their lamps at the doomed Silksworth colliery, one of County Durham's best-known mines*

▶ **Coal not dole** *Striking miners in the 1970s*

◀ **Mine fall** *The end of the tunnel of Coalcleugh mine at Allendale, where miners are busy clearing a fall about half a mile in*

◄ **Banners and pride** Thousands of miners, their wives and children move in procession to Attlee Park, Bedlington, for the annual Northumberland Miners' picnic in the 1960s

▼ **Seventies sights** Bedlington Miners' Picnic and youngsters dance in the main street

Comic character Durham Miners' Gala July 21, 1951 and 'Mr Universe' Lawrence Dutton amuses the crowds

Remember When

Your memories. Your stories. Your history. The Chronicle's Remember When platforms deliver the best in North East nostalgia. Daily, weekly, monthly. Our amazing archive photographs tell the story of how we used to live and remind us of how the world looked. Never mind the rose-tinted spectacles, look back at 'the good old days' with Remember When.

LOVE YOUR HISTORY?

LOVE NEWCASTLE

Are you an expert on local history? Do you know all about things like Tyneside's shipping yards or the story behind the Hoppings fair? If you have knowledge of any specific heritage subject, please get in touch and help play an important part in Britain's biggest-ever media heritage project. With your support, we will be bringing history back to life...

E-mail the Heritage Editor:
harri.aston@trinitymirror.com

LOST
NEWCASTLE

▶ **Market scene** *This photograph, believed to have been taken between 1860 and 1880, shows a young girl selling cordial with meat sellers in an unrecognisable Bigg Market*

Historic heart of a great party city

The Bigg Market has always been packed with pubs but much has changed since the days when the mussel stall was a 'must stop' for any visitor

▲ Sedate scene
The Bigg Market pictured at the turn of the 20th century

Newcastle has become known in modern times as one of Britain's top party cities, which can sound excellent as it brings in much-needed revenue with big-spending hen parties or teams of bachelor parties arriving as lads and lasses, enjoying their last days of freedom, flash their credit cards around and head for the Bigg Market area.

Party-goers are lured from the four corners of Britain and they come just to enjoy the Geordie experience first-hand, lured by the atmosphere of the trendy pubs and restaurants but, on the downside, no-one can fail to be saddened at the pictures of drunken men and women, unable to even walk between pubs without having to crawl at least some of the way.

But this has not always been the case, although this area has always been packed with pubs.

Originally, the Bigg Market was where hirings for farm workers were held, and it became a favourite stopping place for carriers' carts from the country. The large numbers of pubs in the Bigg Market were there to persuade our country cousins to spend as much of the profit from their produce as possible.

In the 1920s and 1930s the Bigg Market was frequently used as a forum where, most evenings, you could listen to the soap box brigade, which included philosophers, theologians and even medicine men of doubtful repute. You could purchase balms and potions or secure, for a few pennies, a racing certainty, straight from the horse's mouth! On a Saturday there would be a large open market, which carried on late into the evening but now has long since gone.

Those that can recall those days will tell of stalls lining the Bigg Market where you could buy anything from soup to nuts while a must stop was always the mussel stall. Parents would sample the mussels while kids could have a penny poke of winkles complete with a pin to take off the caps or, if you were really hungry, you could get a pork dip from the pork shop for just a tanner.

Then there were the ice-cream wars, where, with a couple of traders on the go, the cornets would get bigger and bigger as the evening wore on.

A far cry from today's world where, on most nights, especially at the weekend, mussels and winkles have been replaced by kebabs and burgers. But as party-goers struggle on into the early morning, still looking for that extra drink, they should remember a certain ghost which is said to frequent the area. Apparently, it is the scene of repeated appearances of Ewan MacDonald, the ghostly Highlander who killed a local foolish enough to make fun of his kilt in a pub in 1752.

MacDonald was hanged and his body was sent to the barber surgeon for scientific dissection.

But the hangman had not done his job properly and the startled doctor saw MacDonald come back to life. Ewan was promptly and finally despatched with a heavy tap from the surgeon's mallet.

◄ **Evocative view** A picture of the Old Town Hall in the Bigg Market in the early 20th century

◄ **Well-known landmark** The Rutherford Memorial Fountain in the Bigg Market

◄ **Lively time** The Bigg Market was full of free entertainment in the 1920s and 30s and Saturday afternoons would be full of noise and bustle and a feeling of exuberant life: cheapjacks with croaky voices who attracted crowds and made them laugh with jokes, quacks selling medicines and loud-voiced barrow boys shouting out prices

HUGH.HALE &CO.

HOSIERY WAREHOUSEMEN

GEORGE RYE & S

WHOLESALE & RETAIL

▶ **Proud workers**
George Rye shoe shop in the Bigg Market began trading in 1879. This picture shows the workforce in 1928

24 BAINBRIDGE & C

RISI'S ICES

RISI'S ICES

▶ **Ice work**
Risi's ice cream pitch in the Bigg Market in the 1920s

▲ **Drinking time**
The 1820 engraving of Bigg Market drinkers by Henry Perlee Parker

▶ **Having his say** *A crowd of people listen to a public speaker in Newcastle's Bigg Market on July 13, 1970*

▲ **People power** *The Bigg Market has always attracted the crowds throughout the ages*

▶ **Heated debate** *Street philosophers, preachers and politicians would use the Bigg Market as their platform*

Market place *The Saturday morning market has long since ended in the Bigg Market but this photo shows it in its Victorian heyday*

Watering hole *A general picture of the Bigg Market in 1880 featuring the Golden Lion Pub*

◄ **Feeling flush** *The famous gents toilets in the middle of the Bigg Market, April 18, 1969*

▲ **Old survivor** *The Bee Hive Pub on the corner of High Bridge, August 14, 1989*

▲ **Rooftop view** *The Bigg Market on April 13, 1988*

◄ **Familiar sight** *The monument at the Bigg Market on July 18, 1975*

Gallowgate fanatics
Newcastle United fans at St James'
Park in the 1950s

Heart, soul and lots of passion

The Toon Army is unrivalled in the world of football, with Newcastle United's amazing supporters often making the difference out on the pitch

THEY are simply the best, bar none – the fans of Newcastle United.

Today they are known as the Toon Army, but this is a modern take on Magpie fans who have, frequently in the past, been the extra element that has made the difference in a close match.

It's not so much that St James' Park is a fortress, which it certainly can be, it is the travelling contingent of thousands of noisy Geordies which gives Newcastle fans their reputation and the fact that they follow their team no matter how bleak the outlook is.

In the 1950s, when money was even more scarce than today, and austerity actually MEANT austerity, London was invaded by happy Geordies three times as Newcastle gained their awesome reputation as cup fighters extraordinaire, as they pulled off a hat-trick of FA Cup wins.

But it was games leading up to the Wembley jamborees when the fans made the difference, especially in one famous sixth round FA Cup match on a freezing cold wet winter's day when the Geordies seemed destined for defeat, 3-1 down and being outplayed with 20 minutes to go.

They were not only being battered by the opposition but by the elements as well.

When all seemed lost, it was said that a quiet hum could be heard from the Geordie end of the ground, it got louder and louder and soon you could the hear the words of a song – The Blaydon Races – the words became more audible and louder as every Geordie fan joined in.

The lift the fans got soon spilled over onto the pitch and men playing with their heads bowed soon lifted their chins, they started to move faster, they ploughed through the deep mud with more purpose.

Soon the team were moving as one, moves were coming off, goals came and Newcastle prised victory from the jaws of defeat – and no-one there on that day, Geordie fans or opponents, were in any doubt it was the rendition of The Blaydon Races which changed the game.

Today, it wouldn't be surprising if a rendition of that Geordie anthem would peter out after the first verse, as not many Geordie fans could recite line after line with great conviction.

But it was the spirit of the fans which counted and it is that spirit which lives on today, especially when Geordies see their team up against it and in need of their voice.

The Toon Army spirit is as strong as ever.

▲ **Saluting the effort** *Although the Magpies had performed poorly at Wembley in the 1974 FA Cup final, an incredible welcome home awaited the squad as they returned a defeated team. St James' Park was full - the only thing that was missing was the FA Cup*

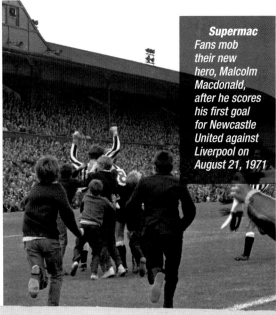

Passionate support Newcastle United football fan at Wembley Stadium for the FA Cup Final in May 1974

Supermac Fans mob their new hero, Malcolm Macdonald, after he scores his first goal for Newcastle United against Liverpool on August 21, 1971

▲ **Toon Army** Newcastle United fans form an enormous queue for tickets on February 24, 1956, with the Strawberry pub visible in the background

▲ **Farewell to the King** Kevin Keegan says goodbye to Newcastle fans for the first time as he retires from playing in 1984

▶ **Going up** Newcastle United 2 Bolton 0 at St James' Park on April 16, 1965, and fans invade the pitch to celebrate promotion

▲ **Glory days**
European excitement reached a frenzy as United took a 3-0 advantage in the first leg of the Fairs Cup final. Fans in the near 60,000 crowd go wild on May 29, 1969

◀ **Special trip**
Newcastle Quayside a few days before the 1924 FA Cup final. United's fans gather for an unusual way of getting to the capital – by steamer down the North Sea. The trip cost 25 shillings for a first-class return ticket

▲ **Immense backing** There was huge crowds at St James' Park as Newcastle fans queued for tickets for the Liverpool game on May 8, 1984

▶ **Going up** Just a small section of the 35,000-plus crowd who stayed on after the final whistle until the Newcastle players returned to receive their acclaim for promotion on May 5, 1984

Sailing to victory The SS Bernicia leaving Newcastle Quayside packed with the Toon Army of 1924. It was noted a 'great crowd gave them a hearty send-off'. It was certainly a different way to get to Wembley

Great scenes *FA Cup winners Newcastle United were greeted outside Central Station by thousands of fans when they brought home the trophy in April 1910*

The heroes' return *Crowds swarm by the Stephenson statue on Neville Street in May 1952*

▲ **We won the cup** *It's May 5, 1952 and the victorious team parade through the streets of Newcastle*

◀ **Local hero** *Paul Gascoigne mingles amongst the fans at St James' Park to watch Newcastle take on Derby on September 28, 1991*

▲ *Back where we belong* Newcastle United 2 Bolton 0 at St James' Park on April 16, 1965 and the fans wait for the players to emerge to a rapturous welcome after gaining promotion to the First Division

City parade More than 250,000 fans filled the streets of Newcastle to greet the returning FA Cup heroes of 1952

Football history with silver-lining

It may be a long wait since Newcastle United last won a major trophy but there was a time when the Magpies were England's top cup-fighting side

Wembley hero Jackie Milburn stuns the Manchester City defence with a goal after only 45 seconds of the start of the 1955 FA Cup final. United won the game 3-1

Newcastle's league success over the years has been a bit patchy, to say the least – and their present-day cup-fighting record is nothing to write home about either. But that has not always been the case.

Every Geordie remembers their Fairs Cup triumph of 1969 when the Magpies beat Hungarian side Ujpest Dozsa to lift the trophy in dramatic style. That Fairs Cup run set Tyneside alight, beating such teams as Feyenoord Rotterdam, Sporting Club of Portugal, Real Zaragoza, Vitoria Setubal and Glasgow Rangers.

In the final, Newcastle went into the second leg in Hungary with a 3-0 lead but things were looking bleak for as the home team went in at half-time well on top and 2-0 up. But as United skipper Bob Moncur famously recalled years later, "Joe (Harvey, the manager), reminded us that we were still 'bloody leading 3-2 on aggregate', then Joe added, drawing on a fag, 'score once and these buggers will fold. They can't stand the pressure. Continentals don't like it!'"

He was right, Newcastle turned it on in the second half and Bobby Moncur himself added to the goal he scored in the first leg with a sweet volley. Dane Benny Arentoft equalised on the night and Alan Foggon, on as a sub, made it 6-2 on aggregate.

This kind of response, of course, should not have been surprising as Newcastle were England's top cup-fighting side of the 1950s, and Wembley (the old Wembley with the twin towers) became their second home.

In 1951, they beat Blackpool 2-0 to win the cup, Wor Jackie scoring twice. In 1952, they beat

cup favourites Arsenal 1-0, Chilean-born George Robledo netting. Milburn was the hero again in 1955 when the Magpies beat Manchester City 3-1. In that game Wor Jackie scored the first goal in less than a minute.

After their Fairs Cup win in 1969 Newcastle struggled on without much success, although individuals such as Malcolm Macdonald (Supermac), Paul Gascoigne (Gazza), Kevin Keegan, Peter Beardsley, Chris Waddle, Alan Shearer, David Ginola and Les Ferdinand had supporters on the edge of their seats with direct and exciting football.

But United rose to prominence again in the 1990s when Kevin Keegan returned, this time as a manager to take up the reins of United. He introduced his own brand of attacking football, brought in some great players and soon Newcastle were, nationally, everyone's second team.

Although they could only finish runners-up in the Premier League, they famously outplayed Manchester United at St James' Park, on live TV and ran out 5-0 winners. The team sparkled that night and the game is firmly lodged as one of the great epic's in the minds of all Geordies. Another game, that United actually lost, is often featured by top pundits as one of the greatest games ever, and that is when they went down 4-3 at Anfield to an excellent Liverpool team.

It was a match which ebbed and flowed, first one team ahead and then the other. Sadly, you could see the pain on manager Kevin Keegan's face as Liverpool scored a very late winner as United were trying to leave Manchester United behind in their chase for the league title.

▲ *Champagne era FA Cup Final, May 3, 1952 and Newcastle United beat Arsenal 1-0 thanks to a late Robledo strike. Joe Harvey, captain of Newcastle United, is chaired by his triumphant team-mates after receiving the cup from Winston Churchill*

Under pressure A high ball eludes Newcastle goalie Ronnie Simpson in the 1952 FA Cup Final

▲ **Pre-war star** Hughie Gallacher in his Newcastle United strip. He is still widely regarded as the finest player in the history of the club

▲ **Goal hero** George Robledo, Newcastle's inside-left, heads towards goal against Blackburn during the 1952 FA Cup run

▲ **Show stopper** Ronnie Simpson is remember by fans for his part in the 1952 and 1955 FA Cup Finals

▶ **Glory strike** George Robledo's header struck the inside of the post and bounced into the goal to win the 1952 cup final

▲ **Back of the net** Newcastle United fans go wild at Wembley when Jackie Milburn scores his first against Blackpool in 1951

◀ **Diving header** Ted Ditchburn, the Spurs goalkeeper, saves a header from Bill Foulkes, Newcastle's inside right, during an FA Cup fourth round game at White Hart Lane in 1952

▲ **Gallowgate favourite**
Newcastle United player Hughie Gallacher in swash-buckling action in 1927 at St James' Park

◀ **Cool finish**
Jackie Milburn equalises in a FA Cup game against Nottingham Forest, in 1955, in wintry conditions

One on one
George Robledo scores against Spurs in 1952 at White Hart Lane

Wonder goal Paul Gascoigne celebrates a stunning goal in the 3-1 victory over Chelsea at St James' Park, with Mirandinha and John Cornwall

▲ **Euro glory** Frank Clark and Bobby Moncur parade the Inter Cities Fairs Cup before delirious supporters at St James' Park

◄ **On the attack** Bryan 'Pop' Robson shoots for goal against Ujpest Dosza in first leg of the 1969 Fairs Cup Final at St James' Park

Action hero *Vic Keeble in action in the 1950's against Spurs with soccer legends Danny Blanchflower and Ted Ditchburn*

▲ **Great leap** *Newcastle goalkeeper Ronnie Simpson makes a spectacular save against Swansea in February 1952*

◄ **Good catch** *Goalkeeper Ian McFaul leaps to gather the ball with Rangers' Colin Stein waiting in vain for any slip-up in the second leg of Newcastle's Fairs Cup semi-final game against Rangers in 1969*

Keen shoppers The crowds out for the first shopping day after Christmas but most of the large stores are closed in Newcastle city centre in 1974

Passion for shopping is true Geordie trait

Newcastle still offers the greatest retail experience in Britain outside of the capital, and this spirit for shopping is deeply ingrained in the people's character

▲ **In the beginning** *A model of the original premises where, 50 years before this picture was taken in March 1932, Fenwick, of Northumberland Street, Newcastle, started. It was to be seen inside the store and attracted the attention of many visitors*

NEWCASTLE is well-known as one of the top shopping centres outside London, and despite the competition from the nearby MetroCentre more than holds its own, bucking the national trend for out-of-town shopping.

In fact, Newcastle boasts the world's first-ever department store, when Bainbridges, then in Market Street and which opened in 1838, began recording its weekly turnover, department by department, in 1849.

But it was the shops of Northumberland Street which made Newcastle such a big draw for Tyneside shoppers when boasting such iconic stores as Fenwick, C&A, Callers, Woolworths, British Home Stores, in naming just a few.

This cavalcade of shops has now been extended throughout the city through the development of Eldon Square shopping centre, which actually starts in Northumberland Street and straddles the whole business area of the town in alleyways which could add up to miles of every different kind of shop you could wish for.

But the most iconic shop in Newcastle must be Fenwick, which opened in 1882 and became one of the largest department stores in the UK. It now has a number of branches, including two in London and one in Leicester.

But the big event in the Fenwick diary which draws crowds of young and old alike, who don't even have to enter the shop, is the annual Christmas window display. In 2008, the *Sunday Times* Rich List revealed that Fenwick was the single most profitable branch of any department store chain in the United Kingdom with assets totalling in excess of £330 million.

Simply known to Geordies as the Toon, which actually refers to the shopping area of the city (a term now adopted by Newcastle United football fans) Newcastle has the vast catchment area of Tyneside to draw from, making it one of the UK's premier shopping destinations.

All towns and cities can tell a dramatic story but Newcastle's must surely be one of the best when, in March 1954, three bears escaped from their travelling cage.

While one was captured near the cage and another in a builders' yard, after a Keystone Cops-like chase, the third caused mayhem as it ran down Percy Street to Eldon Square.

Women screamed and dragged their children into shop doorways, while office workers looking on from above agitated the situation by throwing sweets at the now disorientated bear.

It eventually grabbed one fleeing woman by the hair and dragged her down.

Police inspector SJ Manging dived onto the 6ft bear to get it off the terrified lady. Apparently, the bear merely swiped him away. He dived on the bear again, only to suffer the same fate.

The bear went on to rip a bumper off a car and chase the inspector and fellow constables around the vehicle.

The bear was eventually secured by a heavy rope to some railings.

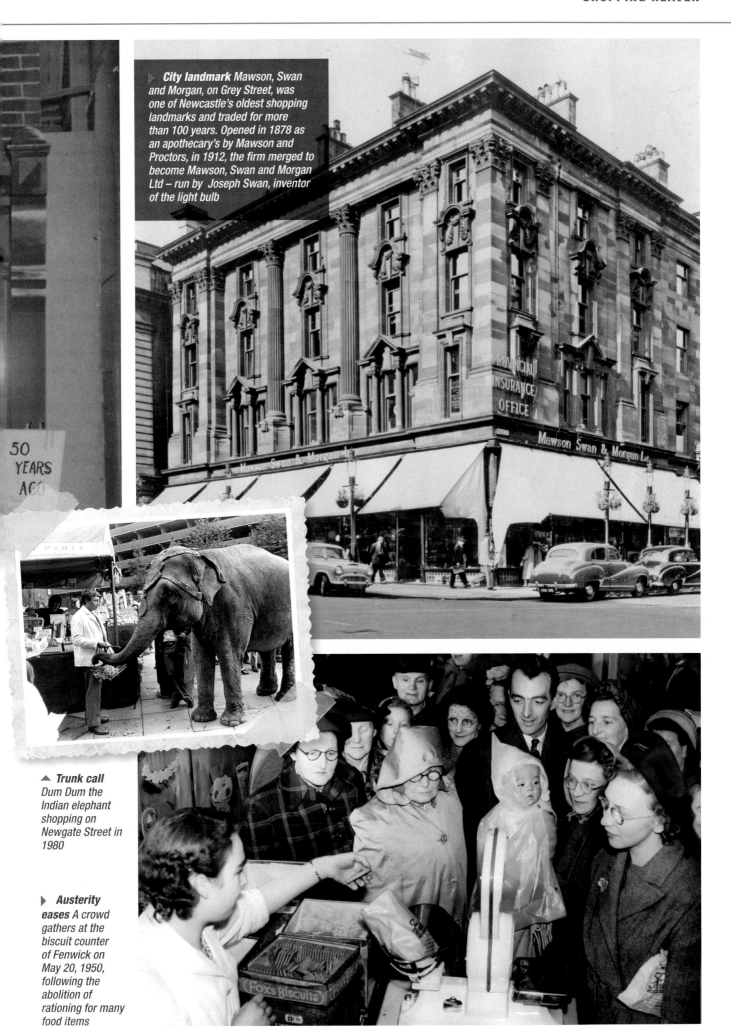

▷ *City landmark* Mawson, Swan and Morgan, on Grey Street, was one of Newcastle's oldest shopping landmarks and traded for more than 100 years. Opened in 1878 as an apothecary's by Mawson and Proctors, in 1912, the firm merged to become Mawson, Swan and Morgan Ltd – run by Joseph Swan, inventor of the light bulb

50 YEARS AGO

▲ *Trunk call* Dum Dum the Indian elephant shopping on Newgate Street in 1980

▷ *Austerity eases* A crowd gathers at the biscuit counter of Fenwick on May 20, 1950, following the abolition of rationing for many food items

Bargain hunters *Customers queue for the start of the Fenwick sale in Newcastle on New Year's Day, 1960*

Crowded streets The present-buying rush reaches a climax in Newcastle on December 19, 1953, as big crowds throng the pavements looking for last-minute gifts

▲ **Great giveaway** Actor Leslie Phillips was in Newcastle on November 16, 1971 starring in the play The Man Most Likely To at the Theatre Royal. As part of a promotion, he was giving out £5 notes to anyone who knew his name at the Co-op in Newgate Street

◀ **Turn of the last century** A market near St Andrew's Church in Newcastle in about 1900

Young entrepreneurs These children host a jumble sale on Elswick Road, Newcastle, in aid of the Evening Chronicle Sunshine Fund in August 1976

▶ **Winter wonderland** This striking winter setting in a shop doorway catches the eyes of hundreds of shoppers on Northumberland Street in 1963

▲ **Night vision** Marks & Spencer on Northumberland Street on December 8, 1970

◀ **Tough choices** These three young ladies just cannot decide which cards to choose for their loved one on Valentine's Day in a Newcastle shop on February 13, 1937

Big draw *Shoppers are out in force in King Street, South Shields, in April, 1949*

▲ **Bring out the bunting** *A scene from Northumberland Street in the 1920s*

Seventies view *The Woolworths and Fenwick stores on Northumberland Street in December 1971*

▶ **Symbol of Tyneside** Work under way on the Tyne Bridge, which is a beacon for Geordies wherever they are in the world

Bridge renowned all over the world

The Tyne Bridge is an icon of the North East and a monument to the brilliant engineers and workmen who laid the foundations of a modern, successful city

▲ Taking shape
Work started on the bridge in 1925 and took three years to complete

IN the mid-1920s it was Tyneside's favourite recreation. Every day the crowds would gather to watch, fascinated, as two giant curved arms of steel crept out from both sides of the river towards each other high over the Tyne.

The Tyne Bridge, opened on October 10, 1928, and stands alone as the symbol of Tyneside. The story of the Tyne Bridge actually goes back to 1860 when plans were submitted to Newcastle's Town Improvement Committee for a bridge occupying roughly the same site as the present bridge.

But these, as did subsequent plans, came to nothing.

Then, from an exchange of letters, in 1922, between a Mr Webster from Corbridge and a Mr Richardson, in the North Mail newspaper, calling for a new bridge, a popular campaign started.

There were 50,000 men without work on Tyneside and any major new project would guarantee many jobs. Finally, in 1924, things at last got under way. Gateshead Council wanted the bridge and Stephen Eastern, Lord Mayor of Newcastle, was determined the bridge would be built.

It was the biggest steel arch bridge built in Europe – three times smaller than its replica, Sydney Harbour Bridge.

During construction a man fell from the bridge, and became the only man to die in the building of the Tyne Bridge.

Nathaniel Collins was married with four children and a scaffold erector from South Shields.

He was working near the top of the bridge which, at that time, was at least 175ft above the river.

It was Saturday, February 18, 1928. The arches weren't more than a few feet apart.

On that fateful day, as the usual crowd of everyday watchers looked on in awe as the "monkey-men" went about their work, Nathaniel must have either slipped or got his footing wrong, because as watchers gasped, he tumbled off the bridge into free-fall.

His body hit the footway on the way down and started spinning like a top until he splashed into the river. Many people thought that a piece of steel had fallen, until the cry went up off the bridge – "Man overboard".

As the crowds on the Quayside and High Level Bridge pressed closer a fellow worker, John Carr, rowed to the spot Nathaniel had entered the water and, as the faller broke the surface, John grabbed him in a vice-like grip.

But there was a strong ebb tide running which meant John could not lift Nathaniel into the boat – but with incredible strength, and with his own life in danger, he hung onto Nathaniel as his sculling-boat was dragged at least a quarter-of-a-mile down river.

People watching said it was a terrific struggle, until another boatman set off from the Newcastle Quayside and helped John Carr to lift Nathaniel aboard his boat.

Nathaniel was then rushed to Newcastle Infirmary where he died.

But the legacy of these brave men is a bridge which is a beacon for Geordies wherever they are in the world.

◀ **Distinctive look** The Tyne Bridge was known as the Mecanno bridge due to its lattice metal span

▲ **In action** Traffic crossing the Tyne Bridge in 1969

Health and safety? Workers on top of the Tyne Bridge as construction nears completion in the late 1920s

Icon is born
The Quayside dominated by the newly completed Tyne Bridge

Job done The mayors of Newcastle and Gateshead shake hands, following the completion of the Tyne Bridge, on February 26, 1928

Three bridges
An aerial photograph of the River Tyne, Tyne Bridge, Swing Bridge and High Level Bridge, September 27, 1972

▼ **Economic success** The bridge, seen here in January 1961, dominates any views of the River Tyne and has proved to be such a success that even its designers, engineers and financial backers would be amazed

▲ **Bridging the divide** The Tyne Bridge, the High Level Bridge and the Swing Bridge in 1936

▶ **Brilliant design** Designed by the engineering firm Mott, Hay and Anderson, the bridge was built by Dorman Long and Co of Middlesbrough. It was officially opened on October 10, 1928 by King George V and is pictured here in January 1966